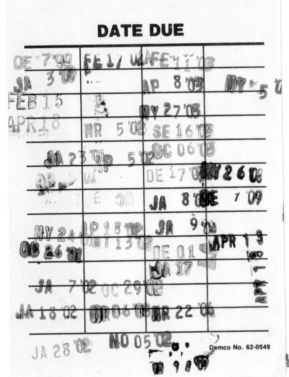

ANIMALS

Owls

by Kevin Holmes

Content Consultant:
David Drake
Coveside Conservation Products

Bridgestone Books
an imprint of Capstone Press

Bridgestone Books are published by Capstone Press
818 North Willow Street, Mankato, Minnesota 56001
http://www.capstone-press.com

Library of Congress Cataloging-in-Publication Data
Holmes, Kevin J.
    Owls/by Kevin J. Holmes.
    p. cm.--(Animals)
    Includes bibliographical references (p. 23) and index.
    Summary: An introduction to owls, covering their physical characteristics, habits, prey, and relationship to humans.
    ISBN 1-56065-603-4
    1. Owls--Juvenile literature. [1. Owls.] I. Title.
II. Series: Animals (Mankato, Minn.)
QL696.S8H566 1998
598.9′7--dc21

               97-14022
               CIP
               AC

Photo credits
Daybreak/Todd Fink, 16; Richard Day, cover, 6, 18
Dwight Kuhn, 12, 14
Charles W. Melton, 20
Root Resources/Alan G. Nelson, 4; Anthony Mercieca, 10
Kay Shaw, 8

Table of Contents

Fast Facts

Kinds: There are more than 150 kinds of owls. There are 22 kinds of owls living in North America. Each kind of owl has its own features.

Range: Owls live everywhere except Antarctica.

Habitat: Owls live in forests, deserts, and jungles. They even live in the Canadian tundra. Tundra is a frozen area with no trees.

Food: Small owls eat insects and mice. Large owls eat rabbits, skunks, and rats. They also eat small birds, fish, and even young deer.

Mating: Owls mate yearly during late winter or early spring.

Young: Young owls are called chicks. They hatch from eggs.

Owls

Owls are birds. They live everywhere except Antarctica. Antarctica is too cold for owls. There are more than 150 kinds of owls. There are 22 kinds of owls living in North America. Each kind of owl has its own features.

Owls are raptors. A raptor is a bird that hunts and eats prey. Prey is an animal eaten by another animal as food. Most owls hunt at night. They are nocturnal. Nocturnal means active at night. Nocturnal owls usually sleep during the day.

All owls have some things in common with other birds. Owls are almost completely covered with feathers. Some owls even have feathered toes. Owl feathers are very soft. This makes the wind pass quietly over their feathers. Because of this owls can fly almost silently.

Like all birds, owls have wings and beaks. They also have hollow bones. Hollow bones make owls light. This helps them fly.

Owls are covered with soft feathers.

Appearance

There are two families of owls. A family is a group of animals that shares features. One family is typical owls. Typical owls have round faces. The second family is barn owls. Barn owls have heart-shaped faces.

Owls can be many colors. Most are gray or brown with some white markings. Colored feathers make owls hard to see. They make the owls blend into their surroundings. It is hard for enemies to spot the owls. It is also hard for prey to see owls that are hunting.

For example, the snowy owl lives in areas with a lot of snow. Its feathers are almost all white. This helps the snowy owl look like the snow.

Some owls have feathers that stick up around their ears. These feathers are called ear tufts. Ear tufts help owls locate where sounds come from.

Feathers make owls blend into their surroundings.

Where Owls Live

Owls live in many places. They live in forests, deserts, and jungles. Owls even live in the Canadian tundra. Tundra is a frozen area with no trees.

Owls choose their roosts carefully. A roost is the place an owl chooses to live or make its nest.

Roosts should protect owls from bad weather. They should also help owls hide from enemies. Roosts must be near food, too. Often roosts are near a forest. Only barn owls choose to live near people. Barn owls hunt in the fields near farms.

Most owls build nests once they have found roosts. Some nests are in trees. Other nests are on the ground. Some owls dig burrows. A burrow is a hole made by an animal as a home.

Barn owls live in the rafters of barns and buildings. A rafter is a beam that supports a roof.

Some owls dig burrows in the ground.

Hunting

Owls' bodies are built for hunting. There are three body features that help them hunt.

First, owls can see very well. Their eyes are large to take in more light. This means owls can see especially well at night. Owls can see prey from far away.

Owls see well, but they cannot move their eyes. They must turn their heads to see things. Owls' necks can bend easily. Some owls can turn their heads three-fourths of the way around. Many can also turn their heads upside down.

Second, owls' wings let them fly quietly. This gives them a better chance of catching food.

Third, owls have excellent hearing. Owls have very large ear holes. The ear holes are covered by special feathers. These feathers do not stop sound. Owls can hear quiet sounds from far away. Owls can even hear animals moving underground.

Owls fly quietly and surprise their prey.

Food

Owls eat many different animals and insects. Small owls eat insects and mice. Large owls eat rabbits, skunks, and rats. They also eat small birds, fish, and even young deer.

Many owls hunt by sitting on a perch and waiting. A perch is a place where a bird can rest. Perches are usually high above the ground.

Owls attack when they spot prey. They stop flapping their wings during an attack. They are completely silent. The owls grab their prey with powerful talons. A talon is a claw.

Most owls return to their perches to eat. Owls have hook-shaped beaks. They use their beaks to tear pieces from their prey. They eat the pieces.

Owls cannot digest hair, bones, or teeth. Digest means to break down food. These items collect in owls' stomachs. The items form balls. The balls are called pellets. Owls spit up the pellets after they eat.

Owls return to their perches to eat their prey.

Enemies

Owls have only a few natural enemies. Eagles and other large birds occasionally attack owls. Sometimes hawks or crows attack sleeping owls. Now and then, large owls attack smaller owls.

Young owls have more enemies. A young owl is called a chick. Chicks often become meals for other animals. Foxes try to catch owl chicks that fall from their nests. Adult owls attack any animals that come near their chicks. Owls have even attacked people.

Sometimes chicks play dead when they are attacked. Some animals will not eat anything that is already dead. Owl chicks lay very still. This sometimes makes their attackers look somewhere else for a meal.

Many animals eat baby owls.

Young Owls

Male and female owls usually live apart. They meet to mate once a year. Mate means to join together to produce young. Owls usually mate in the late winter or early spring.

First, owls must find their mates. Males and females call back and forth to each other. They may do this for several weeks. Then the owls actually meet and mate.

Females lay eggs after mating. Large owls lay two or three eggs each year. Smaller owls lay as many as eight eggs. Female owls keep the eggs warm in the nest.

Males and females work together after the eggs hatch. They feed and protect the young chicks. The chicks eat all the time.

Owl chicks do not look like their parents. Chicks are covered with down. Down is soft, fluffy feathers. They grow feathers when they are older. Chicks leave the nest at three months old.

Chicks are covered with down.

Owls and People

People are owls' greatest enemies. People sometimes pollute the environment. People pollute by making things that release dangerous chemicals. The chemicals can poison the owls' food and water supplies. Owls get sick when they swallow polluted water or food. They often die.

People also destroy owls' homes. Sometimes lumber companies cut down the trees where owls live. Lumber companies then sell the wood. Owls have nowhere to live when the trees are gone.

At one time, many farmers shot owls. They thought owls were bad for their crops. But now farmers know that owls can be helpful. Owls eat rats, bugs, and other pests that damage crops.

Some people are worried because so many owls are dying. They have formed groups to help protect owls.

Owls help farmers by eating bugs and other pests.

Hands On: Test Your Sight

Owls can see very well. They can spot mice from high perches. They can even do this at night. This activity will test how well you can see.

What You Need

A large, open space
One package of multicolored pipe cleaners
Scissors
A watch with a second hand

What You Do

1. Cut the pipe cleaners into one-half-inch (13-centimeter) pieces.
2. Mix up the pieces. Scatter them over the ground.
3. Look at the pieces and pick one color.
4. Have a friend check the time on the watch. You have a two-minute limit.
5. Find and pick up pieces that are the color you chose. Pick up as many pieces as possible in two minutes. Now let a friend try.
6. Count the number of pieces each of you picked up. Whoever picked up the most is the winner. Pick up the rest of the pipe cleaners when you are done.

Words to Know

ear tuft (IHR TUHFT)—the feathers that stick out around an owl's ear

mate (MATE)—to join together to produce young

nocturnal (nok-TUR-nuhl)—active during the night

predator (PRED-uh-tur)—an animal that hunts another animal for food

prey (PRAY)—an animal that is hunted for food

roost (ROOST)—the place where an owl makes its nest

talon (TAL-uhn)—the claw of a bird of prey

Read More

Biel, Timothy Levi. *Owls*. Mankato, Minn.: Creative Education, 1987.

Kalman, Bobbie. *Owls*. New York: Crabtree Publishing, 1987.

Sattler, Helen Roney. *The Book of North American Owls*. New York: Clarion Books, 1995.

Adopt-an-Owl Program
Adams Road, Comp. 18
Site 57, RR 2
Smithers, British Columbia
Canada V0J 2N0

World Wildlife Fund
90 Eglinton Avenue East
Suite 504
Toronto, Ontario
Canada M4P 2Z7

Internet Sites

The Barn Owl
http://www.rain.org/~barnowl.html

The Raptor Center at the University of Minnesota
http://www.raptor.cvm.umn.edu/

Index

16